A Slow Journey to Totality

A Slow Journey to Totality

Poems by

Diane Vogel Ferri

© 2024 Diane Vogel Ferri. All rights reserved.
This material may not be reproduced in any form, published,
reprinted, recorded, performed, broadcast,
rewritten, or redistributed without
the explicit permission of Diane Vogel Ferri.
All such actions are strictly prohibited by law.

Cover design by Shay Culligan
Cover photo by Kate Craine
Author photo by Lou Ferri

ISBN: 978-1-63980-657-7

Kelsay Books
502 South 1040 East, A-119
American Fork, Utah 84003
Kelsaybooks.com

For Lynne
who arrived on the journey just in time

and

In memory of Pam

Acknowledgments

Grateful acknowledgment to the editors of the following journals who first published these poems:

Braided Way: "Under the Milky Way"
Gasconade Review: "For What It's Worth"
Heart of Flesh: "Hiraeth," "Surrender"
Orchards Poetry Journal: "My Aubade"
Smoky Blue Literary: "Old Feminist," "Yellow Lamplight"
Writers Resist: "Election Day"

Contents

I.

Awake	17
You Wander	18
Yellow Lamplight	19
Maybe a Prayer	20
World Without End, Amen (It Still Spins)	21
Under the Milky Way	22
Flinching	23
2:37AM	24

II.

I Am Eve	27
Aging	28
Old Feminist	29
Tipping into the Pink	30
Small Indignities	31
In the 90s	32
The Naked Bodies Were the Last to Be Chosen	33
The Difference	34

III.

Glimmers	37
Election Day	38
The Sixties	39
For What It's Worth	40
What If There Was a Day	41
Well Taught	42
Teacher	43

IV.

Beauty in the Flight	47
The Leaving	48
So Much It Was Red	49
Reading My Parents' Love Letters	50
Forty-Two Years	51
We Should Have Taken Time	52
Grievance	53
Shedding Season	54
Surrender	55
December Lament	56
For Bobby	57

V.

Hiraeth	61
Black Hole Sun	62
Twisted Trees	63
Leaf Time	64

VI.

The Trip	67
Us	68
On the Crooked River	69
Andy's Jazz Club	70
The Art Institute	71
Garlic	72

VII.

Wish	75
Reverie	76
Still	77
Birth Day	78
Grounded	79
Fluidity	80

VIII.

The Whole Why World	83
What Not to Do	84
Luminous	85
Grand	86
Good Blood	87
Flower	88
Glitter Girl	89
We Couldn't Stop Seeing the Leaves	90
Even Still, Children	91
How Little Most Things Matter	92
My Aubade	93

Be not afraid of growing slowly;
be afraid only of standing still.
　　　—Chinese proverb

An awake heart is like a sky that pours light.
　　　—Hafiz

I.

Awake

One year I woke up, which is better than staying asleep.
There is no truth in staying asleep, just nightmares

and dreams you can't arouse from your soul, like
the memory of someone snatching the book out of my

hands as I sought refuge in the school library, preferring
the classics to the conspiracies of the lunch room. A

teacher walked by and asked why I was reading a book
not on the reading list—*because ignorance is a choice,*

I thought. I found my own advantages in the stories and it
was like a song I'd just learned but already knew.

I saw the obstacles and barriers I'd never jumped over
and it was called compassion, reality. I like being conscious

as opposed to the blindness of sleep. Blindness takes one-
fifth of your senses away, not being awake takes all five

senses away. When each morning came and I breathed another
day, I mingled among the races, the creeds, the huddled masses

and was not afraid because love takes nothing from me, it's only
value-added. Mere living brought me into consciousness, and in

the movement of time I understood that my parent's ballot was no
longer mine, that knowing is better than not knowing, acceptance

better than judgement. I began to be *for* things, not *against* them,
to do justly, love mercy, walk humbly with my God.

You Wander

You wander
through your life
as in a snow globe, the glass
holding you in its periphery.

You wander
through your religion
as if it's a building with walls
impenetrable and fixed.

You wander
through the days
in expected expectations,
never moving out of position.

What you learned as a child
is burrowed in like a tick
and cannot be extracted
until you wander somewhere else.

Yellow Lamplight

I hope for a rainy day,
or a snowstorm would be lovely;
for solitary shadows, time to think,
for singing in a loud voice, with
no where to go but the next room.
The gray fog locks me in the house,
the garage door closes in gratitude,
quietude seeps under the doors.
A lamp on in the daytime means
someone is home, not at a
workplace with playground
screaming outside the window.
On my way to teach I wanted
to be the person sitting in the
lamp's yellow light,
reading, drinking tea with milk
in the middle of the morning,
to be wanted but not needed.

Maybe a Prayer

Maybe a prayer is just
looking up once in a while
and seeing the trees like
it's the first time, and
noticing a bird sitting there
doing nothing but waiting.

And maybe a prayer
is having a dream
about your childhood home,
and instead of waking up
crying for what is gone,
you smile in the dark.

A prayer might be only taking
what you need and leaving
the rest for God to handle,
surrendering your heart
with all of your heart,
releasing your soul.

A prayer could be happening
when you are in the presence
of the people you brought into
this world, and then the smaller
people they brought with them,
and knowing you had something
to do with all of that beauty.

World Without End, Amen (It Still Spins)

You don't need to call it God to know what you've known
every day of your life, the movement in your chest, the

pulsing in your toes, the breath that startles you awake each
morning, your body lifting you out of bed like a magic trick.

You don't need to go to a church building or ascribe to a creed
to say *thank you,* but you are welcome to if it moves you forward,

if it brings you into a community, or teaches your children
to be grateful. You don't need to listen to the sanctimonious,

those who create their own truths, but you can allow them to
make up your mind, if you wish. You may revel in the injustices,

or you may choose to be thankful, either way, the rain still falls
and clouds disperse, birds always know how to build nests,

turtles will emerge from the mud, bare branches become full again,
whether you notice the faithfulness of the earth or not, it still spins,

even if you have never given a thought
to where it all came from, why it stays.

Under the Milky Way

I am small enough to sit on the floor
of the back seat behind

my father driving us safely
through the darkest night

my mother navigating next to him
my brother and sister asleep nearby

I search for the spiral of the milky way
that I have heard about but instead

I see God in the stars and it is here
that I learn to pray—not in a church building

the vastness out of my window
is beyond my understanding

and I fall in love with the creator
every time I look up

Decades later I will search for the milky way
with someone who will change me

there will be a song that makes me flinch
that leads me there despite my destination

it will disrupt my beliefs
and cause me to stumble and descend

to never be guileless
to never have the faith of a child again

Flinching

The song is an arrow, a wound
you walk into, then it calcifies in you.

It's a shiver and a jolt, corroding
your existence, making your decisions,

clenching your shoulders, guiding
you in the wrong direction.

You take it in your chest and set your
course to disaster, singing merrily along.

It's fraudulent advice and an alibi for
bad choices. You can pull it out of your ear

but it is a lyrical tattoo, and you may
never stop flinching when you hear it.

2:37AM

A shimmering light shines on my brain, catches
a wave towards morning, a ripple of what

could have happened, of everyone not safely
in their beds, as I am. It moves like a photo-

bomber, foolishly ruining the beauty of
unconsciousness and repose, discharging

out of the mind like shooting stars over
a dark park. Music cuts in, a comfort,

a respite, relentless. I sing, conduct the orchestra,
signal the end of the song with flailing arms, my

fingertips come together in denouement
to no avail. It's on repeat, a song rehearsed

so many times, lodged in an indelible space,
a protection from something more disturbing.

II.

I Am Eve

I make my will known,
improvising in the moment
as women are wont to do.
This choice to be human
is a gift, for what else would I be?

I savor the power of birth,
to bring something forth that never existed.
Give me the pain, make me a mother,
you would not be here without me.

I am unleashed to be all I was created to be.
My eyes are open, my mind is alive.
I am God in the world. I am woman.
Before men wrote my story,
I am.

Aging

My connective tissues are gritty,
translucent, a brush full of rogue
hair, a chest cavity full of loss,
my body is suddenly a sieve, with
loosened scaffolding and Jesus in
my blood. Eclipsed into shortened
days and longer nights, doubts can
cut like a serrated knife, carving
out words of disappointment and
estrangement. I can lay the knife
down and be restored
or keep cutting deeper.

Old Feminist

A new kind of pondering occurs in
the clarity of time and it is not regret.

I wonder why I changed my name twice,
why my eyelashes are too pale, why I

am required to defy myself. I sing in a
lighter voice and each morning is like

coming out from under the water, that
first breath, a complete and satisfying inhale.

I give myself permission to choose
this day and leave the heavy stone

of guilt on the ground. I see it in the young
women and I can afford to carry it for them,

but it's their time, not mine. I want to
tell them that we're never full, that

they're doing it right, it's okay to cry,
and someday time will tip in their favor.

Tipping into the Pink

Once we are entered we're never left alone again,
cut and stitched back together we sidle patiently

toward our desires, but we're never full, we
change our names, think about red stains and

do all the feeding, no, we're not always fine.
We carry the pepper spray, hide the chocolate,

take the blame for Eve—religion does not
favor us. To become the President we must

be flawlessly likable, pleasing to the eyes,
so we bare our arms and legs in cold weather,

eat our awful salads, cover the gray and
wonder why our body parts are up for a vote.

Small Indignities

like paper cuts, multiple paper cuts,
hangnails, stubbing your toe in the

middle of a hot-flashing night, you
defy your age but it keeps returning

to bite you in the saggy ass,
you used to push people out of small

tunnels and feed them while
someone else slept but a man will

explain what a pick-up is even
though you've played the guitar

since you were twelve, and don't cry
because that just makes them feel guilty

color your lips the correct shade and
darken your lashes before leaving home

paint your nails and hide the gray
it doesn't matter because they will

stop turning their heads as you walk
by like a ghost either way

take some hormones, get an
uplifting bra, suck down the

indignities like a good pour
of Pinot Grigio on a hot summer day

In the 90s

The other day I stood in front of the trembling speakers,
vinyl spinning, and tears shattered down my face as if
I'd just heard *Silent All These Years* for the first time,
because *she* was the one who gave me permission.
In the 90s I was doing backbends over my poems, howling
in the night, trying to break out of a methodist existence,
wondering why I'd stayed when the door wasn't even
locked. I was just asking to be alive not a pencil sketch,
scraping the duct tape off my lips, trying to get up off
of my knees, which was easier then. Now I'm a succulent,
I don't need much, I know my eggs are dusty and there
is no bounty on my uterus, but now, at least,
I can hear my own voice.

The Naked Bodies Were the Last to Be Chosen

The young women arrived one by one to exclaim
over what I had to give—my mother's art,

God's way of giving her eternal life on the
walls of strangers' homes. What remained

were all of the nudes in living colors: purple,
green, orange, golden skin tones, the swell

of a child under pendulous breasts, brown flesh
stretched tight with hope, unnameable models,

a man with spread legs in nothing but a do-rag.
Of the homely naked lady with the scrunchy

in her tangled hair, one woman commented
that because she looked content in her body,

her confidence made her beautiful. This young
woman understood the intention, knew the secret:

The eye and heart of the viewer holds the beauty,
and this is the story of art.

The Difference

On a morning news show she
has on a pair of bright red six-inch
stilettos, the heels too long for her to set
her foot flat on the floor from her chair
or her knees would be in her chest.
Her dress is sleeveless, skin-tight,
most definitely some uncomfortable
shape-wear or wires underneath.

He has on a nice suit, arms covered and
a pair of white Converse high top sneakers,
his feet pleasantly resting on the floor,
and that, my friends, is the difference.

III.

Glimmers

They call them glimmers, the opposite of triggers
that shoot you off into hopelessness,

like watching the aftermath of *trigger-happy*
shooters of children in a school or worshippers in a

church, because that is allowed these days for
the angry and lonely. A trigger makes something

happen, whereas a glimmer softens your day in
fuzzy feelings of safety, a faint or wavering light

in the dark. There are warnings before the news,
reports that you may be triggered, so pet a dog,

walk in nature, watch bluebirds at the feeder
and make an earnest plea for the glimmers

to shimmer in you like the sun on snow. Set your
intentions and shine, you only have today, you know.

Election Day

Election day is a carnival ride of hope
and despair, each taking their fluctuating

turns. In the back yard, birds and squirrels
continue coexisting while we, the supposedly

more evolved, battle through every November
and false ad. The downy woodpecker hammers

away at the side of the house and I don't care
because she's committed to her life, she saves some

insects for others and thanks me with her beauty.
I cannot betray the consciousness I've worked so hard

for, so election day terror is like waking up in the dark
as a child and calling for help but making no sound.

All I have now is the sound of a pen making a circle
of black ink on a piece of paper, and these words.

The Sixties

Davy Jones and watermelon candy in my pocket
were all I dreamed of in the '60s, but now I am
in my 60s and they are waning fast. The new
children are growing out of my reach but they
still run into my heavy arms with new information
and innocence, they don't know what's coming
and they don't watch the news, so I relive my youth
with them and it's life's big surprise. In the 60s I wrote
school assignments in cursive with a fountain pen,
outraged at prejudice, war, pollution, political corruption,
just as I probably will today and tomorrow. Classmates
at our reunions are the same kids, just with deflated
balloons as faces, hairless heads, wider hips that birthed
some children, unchanging as the world.

For What It's Worth

The bombing started again—no big surprise,
more separation of mothers and children—

we're not the only country that can pull that off.
Some say it will be world war III but

it doesn't matter what you think about peace,
you're not John Lennon.

As a child I wore a POW bracelet for months
but I never knew whether the soldier came home,

then I lost the bracelet and my innocence.
I remember the day it was over we rejoiced

but we didn't know why,
we just started waiting for the next war

hoping we didn't birth
our sons in the wrong year.

What If There Was a Day

when nothing happened, in between wars and elections,
storms, giant waves, quakes and funnel clouds?

Teams had the day off, strikes were averted, traffic
moved like a dream, thieves and attackers took a break.

Juries were sent home and judges napped, school children
forgot to bully and fight, theater lights darkened, celebrities

tired of their capers. Reality shows were in rerun, mortgage
rates and the stock exchange remained as the day before.

No one was born, no one died. Newspapers had nothing to print,
talking heads stopped talking, all media were muted and stilled.

What if the cadence and rhythms of the planet spun in harmony
and coexistence for just one day . . .

Well Taught

The old man on the elevator leaned
on a walker with a yellow-toothed

grin, I motioned for him to get off
on the second floor before me

but he held his arm out with a
wizened smile, *no please* . . .

As I left the elevator I heard him say,
my father is still watching me.

Teacher

In our humid basement room,
tucked into the stairwell,
I offered a smile, an unfailing gaze,
decades of welcome and safety

to children heavy
with multiple
griefs they could not carry
or disremember.

Then one day
I abandoned them
to journey
alone

through an assembly of other adults
who could start them
or end them.
I took my security with me

after all, I was only meant
to be with them for a season.
A decade on, I still wonder
what happened next,

who loved them
into the future?
What other teacher

set them to fly away
from their invisible wounds,
or did they
never
take off?

IV.

Beauty in the Flight

The pileated woodpecker lands outside
the window, mere feet from my eyes,

startling me with his size and splendor.
I don't move as he hammers at the suet

like a prizefighter pummeling his opponent.
He's wearing a glossy black robe, an electric

red crown—the pileus—this guy's as showy
as a Van Gogh still life. My brain conjures

flying during this birdwatching hour, but not
in a roaring machine where you can't spread

your arms, or revel in your space. It's
bird wings, the release, the view without a

window seat. Now, he's suddenly in flight,
the white lining of his ebony wings flash like

lightning into the twisted, insect-ridden trees,
he's laughing at me from above, watch us fly.

The Leaving

All of the songs are there,
all of the words carried
over. My feet are in the cool
river, feeling the slippery
Ohio shale, as I swim into
hushed deep blue,
I disperse. I am a fish caught
in the eagle's talons, rising up
out of the water, finally
flying, the gorgeous wind
is a color I've never seen.
I glance down and it's an
ordinary Sunday and the choir is in the loft.
(If you are in church do not pray for me,
just sing and I will hear you.)
Particles of other souls
are filling my airspace
and I do not push their softness
away from me as I did below.
My fingerprints are erased and
dreams are becoming logical.
God is there in creation, but
it's the eighth day
and there are other worlds coming.
I cannot find the guilt, the urgency,
the gender of it all,
and it's pure relief.
Face to face I say thank you for
the stars over the Grand Canyon, the lilacs,
El Capitan, the statue of David, the bluebirds,
all of the poems . . .
The earth is a molecule now,
I'm holding gold dust in my hands,
I'll leave a portal open for you.

So Much It Was Red

My mother performed her wifely duties,
pulling clothes from the dryer as I stood

watching, always wanting to be by her side,
and I said I loved her so much it was red.

The moment I wrote this or even remembered it,
is gone, and now another one gone, and so on,

but love, as we know it exists through all the
moments, maybe into eternity—I hope. I hope

there is a great reunion in heaven, as the pastor
said at my mother's memorial service, her body

in ashes on the altar. All that remained were her glorious
paintings displayed in front of us, the songs the choir

sang for her, and my pitiful words to sum up her
well-lived life, her stoicism, her unyielding faith.

Why did I say my love was red? I don't even like
the color red. Did it come from the construction paper

Valentine hearts we made in second grade? The ones
we were asked to give to classmates we didn't love?

Or was it when I first saw my scarlet blood drain out
of my scraped knee and knew it was everything inside of me.

Reading My Parents' Love Letters

They have slept quietly in boxes and envelopes
for sixty years and now are awakened,

the falling in love, *my darling
how happy you have made me.*

She wrote of showing her love for him
by having his baby, and I knew it was me.

The notes and letters accumulate
through all the years and still

I am reading the same thing
you are the best mother, father,

*you are the best husband, wife,
I could have ever spent my life with.*

He wrote *I love you Martha* in the snow
and she took a photograph of it,

he left her notes when he would
leave for early morning golf,

*I will clean this up when I get home,
let's forego the late news tonight, I love you.*

A marriage left to us on aging scrap paper, as if
we had not witnessed this love all of our lives.

Forty-Two Years

My best friend of 42 years died.
I had not known how bad things were,
how a tumor was growing,
shutting down her brain. I'd said
what do you have to do to get out of here?
and no one told me she wasn't getting out of there.
On some visits she'd ask the same things over and over,
on some visits she'd just smile and say *oh wow.*
At the last visit I said,
thank you for being my friend.
We held hands, with one tear on her face
and a faint squeeze she said, *Oh Diane,*
and knew me for the last time.
In that moment only I remembered the 42 years:
four-hour lunches, holidays,
children, grandchildren, together.
My heart is ragged with loss,
scratched open with shock.
I drag out the 42 years of photo albums
and look without comprehension.
How I grieve the first friend to hug me,
how I probably pulled back out of surprise,
how she just kept hugging anyway,
how her laugh soothed me
with 42 years of unconditional love,
even after I egregiously betrayed myself
and she didn't even flinch.

We Should Have Taken Time

It's not a city street, but the charm
of a Cotswold sidewalk, stonework
buildings standing for centuries,
two ladies walking for decades,
trudging the same walkways
in wide-hipped skirts, proper
hats, with heavy shopping bags
on their way to have tea.
The taller lady has a cane,
the shorter one slightly bent over.
I love this painting because
one was supposed to be you
and one was supposed to be me.
But you are not here to walk with me.
You will never need a cane
because you walk on a different
stratosphere, one I am traveling
towards but cannot reach, just yet.

Grievance

I'm not sure if I hate the smell of lilies
but I know I despise them. They filled

the house like a ghost because we had
brought death home with us. They carried

their sorrow with them, a burden, a weeping
headache. We did not need a reminder of what

we had seen, of what had vanished on that
ordinary Wednesday. Days blurred with our fear

of speaking, then one brutal day I roughly grabbed
the beauty and filled a trash can outside, where their

ugly fragrance could not send grief into our heads,
our hearts, places that would never be healed.

Shedding Season

Billowing, rolling across the floor
from the animal that lives here,

I chase the leavings with a useless tool
as we shed together, hair and loss.

But the dog never had to change her name
or bury her parents in the cold ground.

She liberates what she loses on every
surface, in the house, in the yard,

without tears, naturally, she was fixed to
avoid maternal sorrows, but my path has been

more of a straightjacket, fighting the griefs
in my spirit, discarding the fatalities like

clothes in a hamper, ready to be washed,
put away, although I am at a loss to understand.

Surrender

God, hold this breathing body
you resurrected with the morning star,

settle into my shoulder, unclench my neck
while my head breaks like glass.

The same anchor of neurons
that deplete and diminish also

propel my lungs, my arteries
pulsing like mountain streams,

sinews linked and vital
in a brilliant mystery.

What did Jesus do in agony of body
but acquiesce like a guileless lamb,

forgive the thieves, abandon the world,
arise again with the morning star.

December Lament

It's the funeral march towards the end of the year,
just a number, just a month, with joy to the world

and a slithering trail of regrets gaining on me
like a holiday rattlesnake about to strike, sending poison

to the veiny, icy backs of my hands. Visions relentlessly
knock at the frosted windowpane in my mind

not of fairies and plums, but that first wet snowflake
on the windshield, that sudden chord of a song,

a broken ornament, children who are no longer children,
what the year was not, someone who is not here.

Silent snow falls on my winter sorrows, until I look up
from my lament and see God in your eyes.

For Bobby

I never said out loud what was different about you,
it was unspoken then, unnamed in my innocence,

I just knew the girlfriends never lasted long.
The lead role was mine because of you, but yours

was always a bit part—the director didn't like you.
High school plays ended and I left with a yearbook

photo of the only boy in a bow tie,
and all your notes and letters:

I'll always have a special place in my heart for you.
You've given me reasons for wanting to be alive.

I rushed into marriage and motherhood, you went to New York.
Your 8x10 glossy came in the mail *I made it to Broadway!*

Then you were in a nursing home. It was the 1980s. I understood,
foolishly listened to your mother tell me I should not see you.

So we wrote letters, and in shaky handwriting you wrote down
the songs I'd sung so long ago, the ones you'd coached me on.

And then I did nothing. My own life was strewn apart and I did
nothing. I assumed. I was scared. I was wrong. You lived for

a long time and I had not known, or tried to know. I had done
nothing and doing nothing is the one thing I can never change.

PS *You make me feel very special.*

V.

Hiraeth

Welsh: longing for a time that can never be recreated.

Sundays were quiet. I could hear God
and God didn't mind that I stole lilacs

and daffodils to give to my mom and
grandma on the way home from school.

I didn't know the back yard wasn't a
vast forest or why dad scoured the yard

for tiny toads before cutting the grass
with his hand mower. March was the

windy month for kite flying, and cicadas
screamed when it was time to go back to school.

We burned the yellow beech leaves in ditches
and filled our lungs with memories. It snowed

all winter and every day after school we'd pull
our sleds down to the pump-house hill, trudging

back in the twilight covered in crusts of ice to do
our homework at the kitchen table before dinner.

No one believes that God used to speak to me.
Sundays were quiet. Everything was special.

Black Hole Sun*

*Song title by Chris Cornell

The slow journey to totality
forced a swath of our disunited

states to unite for one spectacle
of a day, like nothing in recent

memory, certainly like nothing
on the news. Many thought it

was no big deal but it turned out
to be a pretty big deal, like a day

stopping, like your brain shutting
down for four minutes. Breezes

grew cold, a green light claimed
us in an eerie beauty, a vacuous

moment. As we took off our glasses,
birds quieted, mouths quieted,

a hallucination appeared, we reached
for each other's hands.

Twisted Trees

It is not one tree, but four massive
elderly arms twisting around each other

in desperation. She stares at me through
the kitchen window each morning

like a watchtower, an unmoving mother.
Hollow arms break off in the night,

insects and woodpeckers pockmark her skin,
yet she unfailingly births a mass of cast-offs

swimming through the air, flailing,
accumulating in the wood chips.

I want to resuscitate her, breathe
stamina into her recesses and scars,

ask her how long she's stood there in all of
that dignity, how long will she stay?

I would cover my ears at the murderous sound
of power saws, the crack of a tree falling.

As a girl, I cried in my bedroom window, angry
at my father for killing some baby trees in the

front yard before they could twist up into the sky.
How I beg them to stay.

Leaf Time

It's not just the blazing color or
how you thought the sun was out but

really it was the yellow of the beech trees
coming through the window shades,

and it's not just the smell you can conjure
at any moment, the house filled with

burning leaf perfume, how you'd go to bed and
your pillow was filled with leaves in the morning.

It's not that scritching sound of metal rakes,
a family of rakes on a path to the ditches,

and not the feeling of tired arms, blisters
in the space between your thumb

and forefinger—it's called the *purlicue, but*
the medical term is Thenar webspace—and it's

not just the pile at the end of the slide—
it's the man who put them there,

the man who had no idea he was giving
you a gift to pass along.

VI.

The Trip

In the beginning of this trip
before grief and overgrowth,

I was gamine, you callow, tears rolled
like mercury, silvery and unreachable,

broken for you, holding regrets
in the sinews and ribs.

When a hawk perched on my shoulder
the talons dug deep and bloody, then

it was only gravity that kept me here.
We ran towards desires, without

walking in beauty, moving to planets
orbiting different suns. In this

anthropocene nothing is forgettable,
everything is unfailing, and when

light leaves my eyes, I will still see you,
you will see me.

Us

We are more like one
and less like the past,

your love is silent
I carry mine in words.

In the abundance of winter
you come home

to nothing changed,
and the sparseness

of each day is a comfort.
We are traipsing like gypsies

through this life together,
mended and forgiven

in a sheltering peace.
Leaves fly, snow flies,

blossoms break
and we are still here.

I have loved you
on this ordinary day.

I have prayed for you
on this Valentine's day.

On the Crooked River

Listening to Norah on the river,
boats cluster to hear, people wave
then they're pushed on.
The city washed clean
after the mid-day summer storm.
Towers and bridges lit at the dusk,
white birds soar
and flap to the rhythms.
I smile at him and him at me,
alone in a crowd, come away with me
my heart says to his. Yearning, breaking,
I look up to see
the careless flight
and the birds make me cry.

Andy's Jazz Club

I knew it was perfect when the announcer said
it was a *quiet* jazz club, leave your shouting in the
frigid Chicago winds outside, leave it in your mouth
as you sip your cocktail in the softened lights.

Our table pulled up to the the wooden stage,
like in an old movie, with a view of the masters,
the decades of music written on their skin,
the trombone melodies, the brush on the cymbals,

you next to me in the place we finally found
after so many years of searching, on this
February night, in this meteoric life
we've danced through together.

The Art Institute

Standing among the Renoirs with you,
the bathers in the sunlight, the children

with their shimmering cheeks, the sisters
in their flowering hats, feels right to me.

We are having a moment in beauty
and we are together in this.

Then the huge Seurat, the points of color,
a summer day with parasols. I know how

the brush feels as it dots the canvas.
Once, we traveled to Giverny and stood

on the curved blue-green bridge,
saw the lilies in the burgeoning pond,

and we've seen them in Chicago, Cleveland, too.
The *Nighthawks* still send me shivers, the

yellow light in the stillness, the empty city street.
You stood by the farmer and his daughter

in *American Gothic*—although we always thought
it was his wife. Van Gogh's crooked bedroom,

his self-portrait of multicolored skin, a Tiffany
wall of glassy colors we've never imagined.

Garlic

I don't cook, or love food, or talking about cooking
or food, or watching cooking shows.

Who made this? Here's the recipe! Blah, blah.
Idly, I sit in the corner taking great gulps of wine

at parties, waiting for a break in the droning,
thinking how, at five 'o clock, my mid-century

housewife-mother would disappear into her bedroom
to comb her hair and put on reddish lipstick

so she could serve my father's favorites: meatloaf
and mashed potatoes, bottled gravy, a wedge of iceberg

dotted with a blob of mayo, mushy canned beans,
fruit in heavy syrup. In the mornings she'd pack three

brown bags of white-bread-baloney sandwiches, an apple,
carrot slices, a dime for milk taped inside the bag.

How was I to know what garlic was until I met the man
I love, the one who concocts dreams out of spices

with a chemist's heart and hands, bright orange turmeric,
pale cardamom seeds, the man who can convert cauliflower

into mashed potatoes, squash into french fries, an ordinary
meal into indulgence, a cosmopolitan banquet flowing from

an ordinary galley, as I follow behind wiping up, closing drawers,
scrubbing pots, doing what I do best with my sated, gorgeous life.

VII.

Wish

I wish for a closet full of things I love
and breasts that don't rest on other skin,
I wish not to feel guilty about my nightly
glass and to rise up off of the floor like
a ballerina, I wish for the skin on my
hands to look like a freshly ironed shirt
and to be the girl my mother painted
in her yoga leotard and perm. Sometimes
I wish to go back to riding my bike
everywhere with lightning bugs in my hair
and live in the innocence again, but mostly
I wish to stop wishing for the past and
just watch the children grow, wishing
only for a better world than this one
for them to live in.

Reverie

i dreamed about my son
who is far from me
we clutched and forgave
at the same moment
his runner's heart pumping
into mine

i dreamed about my daughter
who stayed at my side
in feminine devotion
like complimentary colors
our mother-hearts entwined
forever

Still

A tiny diamond in a cheap setting
was not what she should have been

wearing home from the prom. She
knew a lot, but not anything much

about herself or the world waiting
outside of the village. Failures piled

up in stifling stasis and bedridden
dreams until, without warning,

she erupted volcanically, dragging
two children with her through the magma.

She still talks to those children about
what happened and what never happened.

Still, they all try to understand how
she had been so young, how her feet

had been burning in the ruins from the
beginning, still, they talk about it today.

Birth Day

Winter is a lingerer, an interrupter, weeks
of labor pains, hoping any color besides

gray will appear tomorrow, maybe a shred
of blue behind the skeleton limbs of trees.

The paper-whites bloom and shrivel
quickly in the dry-heat air, the iron wind

blows the power away and I'm left to stare
at a deck of birdseed hulls and droppings

until the cardinals and bluebirds bring
their colors with them. When white arrives

I know it's technically not a color, it may
be all the hues on the spectrum, but it's still

beauty in the monochrome. To wake up and see
the bright snow pushing through the shades,

to witness the morning break effortlessly, to
remember it's the day you birthed your baby boy

so long ago, and brought him home
in a snowstorm, held warmly in your arms.

Grounded

He tells me sometimes he leaves
his desk, phone, computer,

walks to the backyard
and puts his bare feet in the grass.

He tells me he runs for miles and miles
through the park in seclusion

where other humans are not.
He tells me sometimes he stops

running and puts his hands
in the ice cold waters of the river,

gleaning what everyone is looking for,
all the answers of the day.

Fluidity

Putting my hands in the eerie lake
I remember the graffiti and the babies

browning in the crepuscular light, my
eyes burning on the sun, on their tender skin.

We brought them to the headlands
to collect pebbles and waves and burns,

lugging bags with tiny shovels, hats with strings.
One baby had been face-up so the doctor turned her,

up to his wrists in the purity of my amniotic waters.
I tried to hide my melon-breasts, leaking

milk everywhere, spilling white down a black
bathing suit, covering myself with a ragged

beach towel. That was when we drank only
sickly blue drinks, listened to only godly music.

The years cooled and drained my reddened eyes
like the thaw after a lake-effect storm,

a storm that arrives like a surprise party
and shuts down the world.

Now I stand behind them on the edge-water,
I walk into the cleansed, fathomless waterways

of Ohio, the serpentine river, I wade
in the shale-laden creeks with new babies,

my head just above the healed waters.

VIII.

The Whole Why World

Mandatory bedtime prayers would
teach them to love the same God I loved,

tucking them into their bunkbed cocoons,
ending with a list of *God blesses,* a chore

to my son, who said, *and God bless
everyone in the whole wide world, Amen.*

When I repeated it one night he said,
No, mom, it's the whole *why* world.

Yes, it is, my son. Like, why our worlds circle
the periphery but never seem to intersect,

why the umbilical cords gave these children
a life but not a faith. Expectations hover

in those indentations we all have
in the middle, even when the shriveled

entwinement has fallen away.

What Not to Do

A beautiful childhood
propelled me into mothering

before introducing myself to me,
I just couldn't wait to have them in my life.

It was all bedtime stories and prayers
until little earthquakes rattled us,

trapping the two children with me
under the rubble, we'd stepped

in the lava, pulled the old maid,
got the wrong side of the wishbone.

The buried wreckage resurfaces again
and again, smacks me in the face

like a wet towel, stinging me to the root.
It's too late to unbury us in this era

when no one says I look too young
to be a grandmother. But they defy sorrows,

they drop their babies into my arms,
and as a redemption I tell myself

they learned what not to do
from me.

Luminous

What magic did I witness
when I was the one to bring

the older child to meet
the newborn sibling?

What other moment in life
could be the sky in my heart?

How we all cried at the sight
of these little humans

meeting the rest of their lives
in a hospital room,

linked together all of their days.
They will dream the same dreams

in their bunkbeds each night,
but recall them as strangers,

like when one sees a starling as
a stubby-tailed brown bird,

and the other sees a rainbow
in its wings.

Grand

Poems are just oozing off of these children
although they don't know how beautifully

obsessed I am. I first fell in love with their
shadows, their surprising soft bones and heads,

when they were nameless and unperceived.
I have found poems curling around ringlets,

in elongated lashes, at the tea party,
in every pile of leaves, every outburst

from a fish caught on the line. How their faces
wound me in the night, I wake up and frame

more photographs, put more holes in the walls,
it's never enough to relive every origin story

or what it was like to be untouched by the world.
I write it all down so they won't forget, so they know

I was always here, and even when the light
abandons my eyes I would never choose to leave them.

Good Blood

Connor

The boy tells me he will eradicate Covid
when he grows up,

and yes, he uses the word *eradicate*.
He has no idea the thrill thrumming

through this teacher-heart,
but more than that,

this beautiful boy has my blood,
if nothing else he is here

in small part
because of me.

I look at this gathering of humans
and where did they come from

if not from the origin story
of two people,

too young,
who did not belong together,

but multiplied nevertheless:
two plus two plus two more.

Flower

Violet

She leaps out from the couch cushions
when I call her name,

yellow ringlets wild upon her head,
sweet-faced beauty as only three can be.

A flash of energy, a romp around the room,
a rush into my arms, clutching me,

clutching something small, something
slightly wilted from an unknown origin.

As she places it in my hands
my heart rises to the ceiling

as if in a dream sequence.
She's given me a tiny flower,

and in this moment she has all
the knowledge in the world,

when everything is simple and true.
This smells like your favorite color, Nama.

Glitter Girl

Lydia

You remind me of all the songs of childhood
with your little-girl group-hugs as you part

ways walking home from first grade.
Your shrieking is a ruckus, shocking

me with its untethered power, growing
footloose despite the world's intentions.

Your imagination tick, tick, ticking,
putting the iridescence in our lives with

swinging cherry-bumps and mile-long
ringlets flinging unbound from expectations.

If this spinning would stop and go
back in time then I would be this good too,

the skipping, holding hands, how we met
your little sister together that one beautiful day.

You might save the world with your exuberance
or maybe with cartwheels across the lawn.

We Couldn't Stop Seeing the Leaves

Ethan

The little boy asked, *why do they call the lion*
the king of the jungle when they live in a savanna?

Oh, little philosopher, you make
all the hallelujahs sing in my head,

you're like waking up with aces,
like all the answers in the universe.

Once, you wouldn't stop crying,
even in my magical arms,

we went outside and you saw the leaves
vibrating in the twilight breeze.

We couldn't stop seeing them, you
and me, your small hand reaching out

for the movement, the light,
putting all the questions in you,

your eyes opening like wings,
it was you flying across my sky.

Even Still, Children

Even with the finger-tapping screens,
the unending amusements, these boys

exclaim over a turtle, a possible movement
under the ice, a bubble coming up

out of the cold—the whole neighborhood hears
their exclamations when there's a fish on the line.

Even with the giant television these girls scream
with glee at the snow sliding off of the roof with

a loud *woosh,* jumping into the *pillow pool*
on the floor, lapping milk from their cereal bowls

with their cat ears on, meowing at me, then getting
ready for the tea party with their little starfish hands.

How Little Most Things Matter

I can't tell my grown children how little
most things matter, they've chosen a side

and it is the right one. They're unaware of
how much wisdom they already hold and

they wouldn't understand how I know this,
so I quietly murmur platitudes of pride,

how they're right where they're supposed
to be. If only they could rest in my words,

but that comes much later—it might
even arrive after I'm gone. I hunger

for them to look my way, but I remember being
in the cocoon they are in now, undertaking

only the day they are living in, loving their
children, making the world right.

My Aubade

I sit squarely in the mercy seat,
having walked there on my knees.
The pages of my good book
flutter to the floor with my affliction,
but then I see the world outside my window
is ironed in white, virgin bright and dry.
Tree branches splinter across the gray sky;
the color of my hair, my skin, my self.
Flakes defy gravity, waltzing down,
spiraling in their silent beauty.
A slash of scarlet lands in a tree
as a descent of woodpeckers,
a charm of finches arrive
in this lotusland,
to redeem this cold morning,
to return me to divine truth,
like a resurrection.

About the Author

Diane Vogel Ferri's full-length poetry book is *Everything Is Rising* (Luchador Press, 2022). Her latest novel is *No Life but This: A Novel of Emily Warren Roebling* (Atbosh Media, 2020) Her essays have been published in *The Cleveland Plain Dealer, Scene Magazine,* and *Braided Way Journal,* among others. Her poems can be found in numerous journals such as *The Orchards Poetry Journal, Blue Heron Review, Rubbertop Review,* and *Poet Lore.* Her previous publications are *Liquid Rubies* (poetry, Pudding House, 2009), *The Volume of Our Incongruity* (poetry, Finishing Line Press, 2018), and *The Desire Path* (novel, Ferri Tales Publishing, 2011).

Diane's essay "I Will Sing for You" was featured at the Cleveland Humanities Festival in 2018. A former special needs teacher, she holds an M.Ed from Cleveland State University and is a founding member of Literary Cleveland. Her poem "For You" was nominated for a Pushcart Prize and a Best of the Net prize.

www.ingramcontent.com/pod-product-compliance
Lightning Source LLC
Chambersburg PA
CBHW030909170426
43193CB00009BA/788